YOUR

INVISIBLE POWER

BY

ERNEST HOLMES

Martino Publishing
Mansfield Centre, CT
2010

Martino Publishing
P.O. Box 373,
Mansfield Centre, CT 06250 USA

www.martinopublishing.com

ISBN 1-57898-931- 0

Cover design by T. Matarazzo

Printed in the United States of America On 100% Acid-Free Paper

YOUR
INVISIBLE POWER

BY

ERNEST HOLMES

Published by

INSTITUTE OF RELIGIOUS SCIENCE
LOS ANGELES, CALIFORNIA

CONTENTS

PART I

GOD, YOUR SILENT PARTNER

•

PART II

GOD, YOUR PERSONAL SELF

The Life That is Within You 7
The Mind That is Within You 9
The Law That is Within You 11
The Power That is Within You 13
The Friend That is Within You 15
The Healing Presence Within You 16
The Peace That is Within You 18

•

PART III

GOD, YOUR IMPERSONAL SELF

I Am That Which I Am 21
I Am Abundance Within You 23
I Am Creativeness Within You 25
I Am the Christ Within You 27
I Am the Sustainer Within You 29

•

PART IV

GOD, THE SELF-EVIDENT TRUTH WITHIN YOU

ILLUSTRATIONS

BY JOHN ARENSMA

I

In The Beginning was the Word, and the Word was Light

II

And the Light Became Law and Took On Mechanical Form

III

And Out of the Light Came Life

IV

And All Created Things Turned to the Light

V

And the Light of Consciousness Dawned

VI

And Man Walked in the Light

VII

And the Light Was All

YOUR INVISIBLE
POWER

●

PART I

I

GOD
YOUR SILENT PARTNER

Part I

E ARE in partnership with the Infinite Mind. The name of this partnership is "God and Company." The supreme Intelligence, the universal Creative Order, the dynamic Law and the all-perfect Presence—this is God, the Silent Partner. We are the Company. This partnership cannot be dissolved for this union was never created—it always has been and always must remain.

We are in league with the universe and this Company, with which we do business, having Its center everywhere and Its circumference nowhere —being omnipresent—is localized wherever thought and consciousness function. Wherever we place our attention, there the Company is doing business. And wherever this Company does business, there is Divine activity.

The activity of right ideas is the Father's business, and the business of the son. That is, the individual mind and the Parent Mind are one, and at whatever point we place our mental attention, at that point the firm of God and Company establishes a branch which is certain to be successful.

God and Company has no competitors. There are no other goods so perfect as those we manufacture. There are no other patterns so attractive. There is no other machinery so noiseless, perfect and efficient. God and Company, therefore, never deals with competition but always with completeness. Wherever our thought is, there this Company establishes Its branch.

Each branch carries an entire stock of the Divine Goods, and we need have no sense of a monopoly of any one of these goods. What mathematician would deny to anyone the privilege of using the principle that two and two make four? Or what musician would claim that the particular note he struck used all the harmony? For the mathematician uses the principle of mathematics and the musician uses the principle of harmony, and

a principle is that which, no matter how much it is used, is neither less nor more than it was. It always refuses to be anything except exactly that which it is, and it is what it was, and it was what it is. And when tomorrow shall come it will still be that which it is.

With God and Company business is always good. To know this is to know the truth about one's business, to understand what is exactly so about one's profession, and to know what activity really means. Who would dissolve such a Divine Partnership as this? If we have a business which has no competitors and over which there is no monopoly; if we have a business that is always good, always active; if we have the intelligence to run this business; and if this business is really the business of living, then indeed we are successful.

In actual practice we must claim this Divine Partnership; we must claim that we are a member of this firm of God and Company, that the business of life is good—active, happy, whole. We must learn to counsel with this Silent Partner of ours and to accept His guidance. When we realize that our Partner makes things out of Himself by Himself becoming the things that He makes, then we shall know that no matter what undesirable facts may be in our present experience, He can dissolve them for us. Thus we transfer our burdens to this Silent Partner who has no burdens and who has no problems.

YOUR INVISIBLE
POWER

●

PART II

II

GOD
YOUR PERSONAL SELF

Part II

THE LIFE THAT IS WITHIN YOU

HE LIFE within you is God, whatever is true of God is true of your Life, since your Life and the Life of God are not two, but One. The enlightened have ever proclaimed this unity of good, this one-ness of man with God. For this reason many have spoken of this Life within you as both personal and impersonal. Impersonal from the standpoint that It is universal — personal from the standpoint that this Universal Life Principle is personified IN you.

This Life within you, being God, did not begin and It cannot end, hence you are immortal and eternal; that is, you can never be LESS, but must forever be MORE yourself; as this Life within you unfolds through your experience, through your gathering of knowledge and your accumulating of wisdom. Evolution is the DRAWING OUT of the God-Principle already latent within you. It is this God-Principle within you which Jesus referred to when he said, "Before Abraham was, I am," and when he said to the one who passed from this life with him, "Today shalt thou be with me in paradise."

The God that is within you is truth, beauty, harmony and wholeness. Every apparent imperfection from which you suffer is a result of ignorance. Because ignorance of the law excuses no one from its effects, it follows that the very power which has bound you, RIGHTLY UNDERSTOOD AND PROPERLY USED, will produce freedom.

The God within you is a Unity and not a duality. The very fact that this Unity is changeless, forever revealing Itself to each, is why the God who is already within, even though He is harmonious and perfect, has ever appeared as the God we believe in. We might say that the God within, being Infinite, appears to each one of us as the God who is believed in. And we worship the God whom we believe in, rather than the God who

7

IS. But there is nothing wrong about this, since the God who is BE-LIEVED IN, is, at all times, some part of the God who IS. Therefore, whatever God you believe in, provided you believe this God is already in you, must respond to you at the level of your belief. This is why it is done unto each one of us as we believe. The Principle is infallible; the practice is what we make it.

There is a great difference whether or not you believe God to be within you or outside you. For if God is outside you, how are you going to reach this God, who, not being some part of you, must be separated from you? How can you hope to unite things which are different from each other? But the God who IS ALREADY WITHIN YOU, being forever perfect and complete, needs no reunion with anyone and you need no reunion with this God, because this God already is in your every act, in every thought, in every movement, in your every plan, purpose and performance. The God within you creates every circumstance and situation you have ever experienced. You have called these circumstances and situations things in themselves, but they never have been. They have always been the fruition of your thought, and your thought has always been dominated by your belief in God, that is, ever since you have had self-conscious life.

Ever since you have had self-conscious thought, you have, by your use of the law of liberty, created bondage. Not that bondage really existed, but the possibility of using freedom in a limited way existed. You really never BOUND freedom, you merely used it in a RESTRICTED way. The restriction was not in the Principle, but in your use of It. There is a difference whether you believe in actual limitation, or merely in a restricted use of freedom. If limitation were a THING IN ITSELF you could not change it, but since it is merely an outline of experience, why not use your imagination to enlarge that experience. When you do this you will find the Life Principle within you responds just as quickly to a broader outline. The old outline was IMAGINARY only, NEVER REAL. It was like the horizon where the earth and sky appear to meet, but as we travel toward this apparent wall, we find that it disappears.

Whatever you mentally see and spiritually comprehend, you may objec-

tively experience, for the God within you is not limited to any one experience. It is the Creator of all experience.

THE MIND THAT IS WITHIN YOU

Emerson said that there is One Mind common to all individual men, which, of course, means that the Mind of all men is the One Mind which each uses; therefore the Mind which you use is the Mind which I use, It is the Mind which everyone uses. It is the Mind of God and because the Mind of God is a complete unity, It is omnipresent. Therefore the Mind which you use and which is your mind now, is the God-Mind in you—this Mind is in all people, envelops all and is at the center of every thing. This is why it is that when you know the Truth at the center of your own being, you know it within the only Mind there is. This is why we are told to "let that mind be in us which was also in Christ Jesus." That is, the Mind which you possess at this moment is the Mind which Jesus used to demonstrate the Christ Principle. He must have realized God at the center of his being, and it is a realization of this Mind of God at the center of your being which gives power to your word.

Since the Mind within you is the Mind of God, and since the Mind of God has been in all people, then it follows that the intelligence within you understands what the great of the earth have been talking about. You already have within you an understanding, a comprehending mind. The Mind of God has no problems, no difficulties, and is never confused. Therefore, your real mind has no problems, knows no difficulties, and is never confused. It is your intellect which is confused. When you know that the Mind within you is God and cannot be confused, then your intellect becomes clarified.

This Mind, which is God, permeates every atom of your being. It is the governing Principle in every organ of your body. It is the Principle of Perfection within you. Your thought is the activity of this Principle. The Principle is perfect, complete and limitless, but your thought circumscribes Its action and causes the very Mind of Freedom to create conditions which you call bondage. As you teach your intellect to believe in the free circulation of Spirit through you, then your thought becomes a law of elimina-

9

tion to congestion, it purifies stagnation. Your consciousness of the Divine Presence within you, like light, dissipates the darkness. This is your eternal and true self at the center of your being. It is the Mind of God manifesting Itself in you, as you. This "you" which It manifests is not separate from Itself, but IS Itself. This Invisible Presence is the Cause of your personality, the light shining through it.

The Divine and Infinite Mind, always desiring self-expression through you, is an insistent urge compelling you to move forward. The Mind in you is also in all people. When you recognize other people, it is this Mind knowing Itself in them. This Mind within you is timeless, yet It creates all periods of time. It is the intelligence back of every action, whether you call such action good, bad or indifferent. It is always creating form, but It is never limited to any particular form. It is in your every act, but It is always more than any or all of your actions. Even though you appear to be bound, the Mind within you is perfectly free.

Your intellect in no way limits this Mind merely because it conceives of what you call a small form or a little space. It could just as easily conceive of what you call a large form or a bigger space. In other words, your intellect is doing the best it can with the Mind within you. It reflects this Mind, but not completely. As the Apostle said, "Now we see through a glass darkly." That is, the full glory of your Christ-consciousness does not yet appear at the surface; only a dim shadow or a faint echo of It appears. Therefore you are the Eternal Mind, not caught by time, but manifesting Itself through time. You are not, then, merely a shadow of this Mind; you are really the substance of It, you are this Mind in action and the enforcement of Its Law. This Law is the Law of your Divinity, and since you are an individual, you manifest this Law in a unique way. You project this Mind through experience in a personal manner, different from all others. This constitutes your true and immortal self.

Since the Mind within you is the Mind of God, and since the Mind of God not only created everything that has ever existed, but will create everything that is ever going to be, you already have within you the ability to project new ideas, new thoughts, new inventions. Therefore, whatsoever ideas you desire, when you pray—that is, when you listen to this inner

Mind—know that you are going to receive these ideas, for you are dealing with that Mind which is the Conceiver of all ideas. When you call upon this Mind for an answer to your problem, It at once knows the answer because there is no problem to It. In this way the answer to every problem already is in the Mind which you possess. "Beloved, now are we the sons of God."

THE LAW THAT IS WITHIN YOU

The Law that is within you is an activity of the Mind Principle in you. This Mind within you is the Mind of God.

All inquiry into any truth, whether we consider such truth physical or metaphysical, leads to this inevitable conclusion, that the final creativeness of the universe is a movement of intelligence within and upon Itself. This Intelligence already exists at the center of your own being. It really is your own being, and the very power of imagination which you exercise is this Intelligence functioning at the level of your comprehension of It. To think is to create.

The Law that is within you is both universal and individual. Since your mind is some part of the Mind of God, there is a place within where you are universal, where you use Universal Power. That Power is Law. This Law, which is at the center of your own being, no doubt you have used largely in an unconscious way; that is, you have used It in ignorance of Its true nature, consequently, the very good which you so greatly desire, but which you have been afraid you would not gain, has been kept away from you because you have denied its presence in your experience. To affirm the presence of this good is to use the Law within you for the creation of this good which you affirm.

One of the most fascinating things which you will ever learn is that this Law, which exists at the center of your being, is creative; that you use the same creativeness which brought the planets into being, the same creativeness which produces everything that is. The Law of your life is really a law of freedom, but you have used It as a law of bondage. You must now use It as a law of freedom. All individual minds, your own included, are merely different activities of the Infinite Mind. This Mind of

11

God is the Law of your life. When you speak, It speaks within you. Thus your thought becomes the law of your life because the Law of the One Mind already resides at the center of your being.

To think is to create. You have already been thinking and creating. Now you wish to create good instead of evil, abundance rather than limitation. You have this possibility within you, for the Law within you is set in motion by the Mind within you. The Mind within you is God, having complete authority over the Law, but you must reverse your use of this Law. You must accept your freedom, announce your liberty and proclaim your Divine birthright.

Whatever you believe to be true about God, declare to be the truth about yourself. Know that the Power within you, which is God, is the Law of Good, establishing right action in your life. In this manner you will gain dominion and exercise authority.

To think is to create. A thinker is a creator. He lives in the world of his own creation. You are a thinker; therefore you are a creator. Consequently, you live in a world of your own creation. At first this doesn't seem to be true and you may deny it, but finally you will come to see that if this were not true, you could not be a free individual. If it is true, then your very bondage is a result of an ignorant use of your freedom.

To think is to create. This is really the key which opens the doorway to wisdom and power. That doorway is already within you. Somewhere within you the Mind of God reveals this truth, that you were born free, that the will of God for you is one of goodness, truth and beauty, that all the power there is, is for you, and all the will there is, wills life. You are the image and likeness of this Life; you are a personification of It; you are the personality of God. The Kingdom of Heaven is already within you and the Law of that Kingdom is harmony, peace and joy.

But if this Law of God within you is one with the All-Law, then there is no opposite to It, nothing can contradict Its final, absolute, supreme authority. You must know this. And in knowing it you will exercise that authority which the Eternal Principle has incarnated in you. But if to think is to create, thoughts are things and the law of things is a law of thought. Change your thinking, then.

12

III

This will not be easy at first because old thought habits are prone to reassert themselves, to claim they have a right to remain in your consciousness, to harass and torment you. But now you are wise and you know they have no such authority. You see them to be exactly what they are—false impressions claiming to be the truth. They are traitors to your True Self, false representations of the Divinity within you. They are a misuse of your law of freedom, but you will cast them out. You will say to them, "I no longer accept you. Begone!" And because they are only thoughts, they will evaporate.

What a wonderful thing to realize that this Mind within you is also the Law within you, and that the Spirit within you, which is God, acts through this Mind, upon this Law, at your direction. You should rejoice that at last you are awakening to this realization of truth, that there is no law for you but your own soul shall set it, in the one great Law of all Life, Truth, and Wisdom.

THE POWER THAT IS WITHIN YOU

The Power that is within you is the power of your word. This Power is not so much a will, as it is a willingness; that is, you will never have to WILL things to happen, you will merely have to KNOW that they are happening.

This Power as Law, which is within you, is neutral and impersonal. You are not to think of It as though it were God, for the Law of Mind within you is merely a mechanical force which you may use for definite purposes. Hence, it is no more God than electricity is God. It is the reaction of the Law of Cause and Effect to your word. This Law of Cause and Effect is merely a way, a medium. It is an all-powerful medium and an all-perfect way.

You have been exercising an authority and a power over this Law through your word, but, you were not entirely conscious of this word because this word was just as much subjective as it was objective, it was more or less unconscious, rising out of race suggestion. You are not to think of the Power within you as a person. It is merely a principle, It is a principle of nature, a law of cause and effect, a medium.

You have the power to use this medium in any way you see fit. There-fore you have thought that the law of your being was one of bondage. Now you are going to discover that it is freedom. Just as it was discovered that the law which causes a piece of iron to sink will cause an iron boat to float, so you will discover that the very law which has produced discord in your life can as easily produce harmony.

Therefore you will not be using two powers, but one Power in two different ways, and experience has already taught you the better way to use this Power. In other words, you wish to use this Power to produce happiness and success, joy, love and friendship, rather than their opposites. You wish to make iron float by the very law which made it sink, that is, you are going to reverse your mental position, for this is your authority in the law. You are going to realize good instead of evil. You are going to use your authority in the Law to create beauty, peace and joy. They will re-spond just as quickly as the more ugly manifestations have responded, and you are going to have the greatest satisfaction which can ever come to you —the satisfaction of knowing that you are really a free mental agent in a spiritual universe which holds nothing against you but which always de-sires your good.

No greater good can come to you than to know that the Power already within you is the power to live, the power to create. Not only to create for yourself, but for others—the power to do good, the power to heal, the power to prosper. You are to realize that the Power within you is a Di-vine Authority. It is a dispenser of the Divine Gifts. It is a giver of life, of joy. It proclaims the Kingdom of Heaven, the harmony of the soul and the unity of all being.

This Power within you responds definitely to direct, conscious thought. It responds as a mathematical and mechanical law of cause and effect. No one can hinder your use of this Power since It is an immediate presence at the center of your own being. No one can reverse your use of It since nothing can contradict Its authority. Therefore you not only have some power at the center of your being; you have access to all the Power there is at the center of your being, to all the Presence that there is, and to the only God there is.

14

You must begin to contemplate this Power within you as answering your every need, supplying your every want, fulfilling your every wish; and you must believe that It does this immediately, right now—not tomorrow but today, because the Law of this Power within you knows no time. Therefore, when your word directs the Law within you, it must always direct It for today. You must give conscious direction to this Law and you must definitely expect It to respond. When you say to the Law within you, "Do this!" you must know It is going to do it; you must believe, there must be no doubt in your consciousness. For the Power, Presence and Law are one and the same thing, and the creative imagination of your own thought is the dictator of your destiny.

THE FRIEND THAT IS WITHIN YOU

You have a Friend within you who is closer than your shadow. This Friend anticipates your every desire, knows your every need and governs your every act. This Friend is the God within your own soul, the animating Presence projecting your personality which is a unique individualization of the Living Spirit.

This Friend within you is Infinite, since He is a personification of God. He is not limited by previous experiences which you may have had, by present conditions nor passing situations.

He has no inherited tendencies of evil, lack or limitation. He has never been caught in the mesh of circumstance. He is at all times, radiant, free and happy.

To your intellect this invisible Friend may seem to be someone else, not your Real Self, but such is not the case. Some have believed that this Friend within you is a mediator between you and the Creative Spirit. Others have believed Him to be the reincarnation or the re-birth of your previous self, while still others have sincerely believed Him to be some discarnate soul. But you are not to accept such beliefs for the Real Person within you is a direct personification of the Universal Spirit. He is your inner, absolute and perfect Self.

The Friend within you is different from all other persons, yet He is united with all. There is some part of you which reaches into the nature

15

of others, thus irresistibly drawing them to you and drawing you to them, binding all together in one complete unity. Right now you are one with all persons, all places, all events.

The Friend within you lives in a state of poise, He is above fear, He is beyond hurt, He is sufficient unto Himself.

The Friend within you is continuously looking after your well-being. He always wishes you to be happy, to be well, to be radiant. Being the very fountain of your life, this Friend is a luminous Presence, evermore emerging from pure Spirit, evermore expanding your consciousness. He is the High Counselor, the Eternal Guide. He is your intellect, the essence of its understanding, the nicety of its calculation, the appreciation of its temperament.

There can be no greater unity than exists between you and this inner Friend. He spreads a table before you in the wilderness of human thought. His cup of joy runneth over. He laughs at disaster, triumphs over human failure, and mocks the grave. When this present experience shall be rolled up like a scroll, He will pass on to new and greater experiences. But to-day He is here. Trust Him, then, today, and you may trust Him for all the tomorrows yet to come. Thus your "tomorrow and tomorrow and tomor-row" will be but an expansion of your endless today.

Your personality is an outpicturing of the impressions which you have received from this inner Friend, this Deep Personality, this Radiant and Divine Presence whose Life is light, whose Consciousness is peace and whose Presence is power. You are an incarnation of this Person, this Presence and this Power.

Possibly it will be difficult for you to believe that there is such a Friend, but He is there at the very center of your being, directing your thought and causing you to triumph over every defeat, for He is an unconquerable hero. He who keeps silent watch within you, lifts your consciousness to the real-ization that you are forever protected, forever safe, forever perfect.

THE HEALING PRESENCE WITHIN YOU

There is a Healing Presence within you. This Healing Presence you must recognize before It can operate for you because, like every other thing in nature, It works according to exact and mechanical law.

16

The God who is within you has already created this marvelous mechanism, which you call your human body. The Intelligence which designed and projected this body must have a perfect knowledge of all its parts; must have a perfect understanding of all its needs, and It must be able to rebuild those parts and supply their needs. The Creative Agency within you knows how to re-create. But this Healing Presence, being the very essence of your own nature, must flow out into action through your consciousness of who and what you are. Hence you must recognize the Great Healer, the Divine Emancipator from physical bondage and pain, as your true Spirit.

Since the only final creative agency in the universe must be Mind, and since you are Mind, it follows that this Healing Presence performs Its beneficent act through your consciousness. This is why it is that you have always been told to believe. Therefore if you wish this Healing Presence to manifest Itself, you must believe that It WILL do so, and having believed that It WILL do so, you must state that It is doing so for it naturally follows that It can do for you only what It does through you.

You must believe in the Healing Presence within you and within all people and then you must speak your word in such a way that this Healing Presence may, as It flows through that word, perform the miracle of life which is the giving of form to the invisible. Your word, then, must be definite, conscious and concrete. You must know that the God within you, as a healing presence, is now the law of perfect life in your physical body. This Healing Presence is reforming your physical body. Continuously It is re-creating all of its parts.

The only way this Healing Presence can create for you is through the images of your thought, through the beliefs which you entertain, whether these beliefs be hope, fear, doubt, faith or failure. Therefore you must correct all beliefs which deny this Healing Presence. In fact you must go so far as to deny that there are any negative agencies and to affirm that the Life Principle within you not only destroys all fear in your mind, but dissolves every object of fear in your physical body.

If you succeed in healing your thought, then this Healing Presence will heal your body as It flows through the new thought pattern. For every denial of physical wholeness, then, you must supply an affirmation of your faith

17

and confidence that the Spirit within you, being perfect, acts as a law of wholeness to your body. Your body is a body of right ideas. The Healing Presence within you, flowing through all these ideas, lubricates them with the oil of gladness and makes perfect every organ, every function, every action and reaction. The Healing Presence within you already is perfect and it is your recognition of this Perfect Indwelling God, which makes possible the execution of the Law of wholeness.

The Healing Power within you, being the same Healing Presence within all people, may not only become the law unto your own individual physical experience, but you also may use this God Power within you to help and heal others. And since everyone exists in the same medium of Mind, when you desire to speak your word of healing for someone else, you should first recognize the Healing God who is within you, after which you should recognize the same Healing Presence within the one whom you wish to help. Then you should make your direct statements for him as though he were yourself. Your statements about him, then, will become the law unto him just as they have become the law unto yourself, establishing harmony in his physical being. State that your word is the law unto him; that it removes doubt and fear from his consciousness, and with the disappearance of doubt and fear there will be a corresponding disappearance of their manifestation.

The more you use the law of this Healing Presence within you the more completely aware you will become of Its effectiveness, and the more certain you will be that it is not I, "but the Father that dwelleth in me, he doeth the works."

THE PEACE THAT IS WITHIN YOU

God is Peace. This Peace which God is belongs to man and is some part of his spiritual nature. Whatever God is in the Universal, man is in the particular. The nature of God is incarnated in every living soul.

The Peace that is within you is not something separate from God. It is not something that bombards you from without. This Peace is something that expands from within. Always this Peace has been in you. Always this

Peace has nestled at the center of your being, ready to reveal Its perfection and harmony.

Peace stands at the door of your consciousness and awaits your acceptance of It. However, It does not stand outside your door, waiting for entrance, so much as It stands inside waiting to be expressed in everything you do. If the possibility of your peace were dependent upon some external event, some outside circumstance, some objective fact, then you would not have a Principle of Peace within you. You would merely be hoping that one might either develop or be imposed externally.

"The Kingdom of Heaven is within you." Within you is the Kingdom of God and within the Kingdom of God is Peace. A conscious knowledge of this Peace, coupled with a definite use of the Law of Mind, gives to each the possibility of freedom from the bondage of doubt, fear and uncertainty.

Peace is within you now. The Peace that passeth all human comprehension is there. The Peace that is at the very heart of the Universe is there. The Peace that said to the waves, "Be still!" is there. The Peace that healed the lunatic of his obsessing thought is in you. Peace is within you now—the Peace that stilled the tempest and walked the turbulent waters of human discord.

Because God is Peace and because God is in you, the Peace of God must also be in you. You should no longer go in search of Peace, for this is confusion. Search Him not out, but seek Him at the center. He has always been there. Did not the Spirit of Truth, speaking through the understanding of one who realized the Divine Presence, say, "Before Abraham was I am"? And, "Destroy this body and I will raise it up again"?

Because Peace is within you, It is available. If It were somewhere else you would never find It. Act as though Peace already possessed your soul and It will possess it. Act as though Peace already emanated from your spirit and It will emanate from it. Speak Peace into confusion and your peace will heal that confusion. This healing power is to be used and not merely believed in. There is a vast difference between believing in a principle and using it. To believe in and understand a principle is essential

to the use of it. But to believe in and understand a principle is merely preliminary to the use of such a principle.

Peace is at the center of your own soul, it is the very Being of your being. This Peace, which is at the center of your being, has never been disturbed. It has never been afraid. It never desired to harm anyone, therefore it never has been hurt. How, then, shall you use this great gift which nestles at the very center of your being? You are to use it consciously. You are to speak the Word of Peace wherever discord appears. And when you do speak the Word of Peace, let no doubt arise in your thought. You must know that Peace stills the tempest. You must know that your Peace has all Power because It is the Peace of God within you.

The Peace which is at the center of your being was not born from human struggle, evolution or accomplishment. It is something that always existed. It was not given by the world. The world cannot take it away. It remains perfect, exactly what it always has been. It awaits your recognition that you may enter into conscious partnership with It. And when you have joined the forces of your intellect with Its infinite calm, then your heart will no longer be disturbed, nor will it be afraid.

Above the wind and higher than the whirlwind, enshrined in the
Heart of God, there is a Voice within you which says:
"Peace! Be not afraid. It is I." This "I" is YOU.
This "YOU" IS GOD WITHIN
YOU. This God within you
IS Peace.

YOUR INVISIBLE
POWER

●

PART III

IV

GOD
YOUR IMPERSONAL SELF

Part III

I AM THAT WHICH I AM

AM THAT which I Am, I Am the Eternal Presence of your own Self. Thus there is no mediator between you and Myself but your own thought. This I Am has been revealed to you in innumerable ways through the inspired writings of the ages. Each inspiration has been a proclamation that I Am is in the midst of you. I Am the writer, the inspirer, and the thing written about. I Am the Creator of history, the One who experiences it. I Am its record and its interpretation. Everything which has ever transpired has but symbolized My Divine Presence at the center of all.

I Am within you is the only Presence there is. I create innumerable centers of My Consciousness, personified as people, yet I Am is the thread of unity running through all, binding all back to Myself. Because I Am a Perfect Oneness, all of Me exists everywhere. Therefore, wherever you recognize Me, there I Am. And whether or not you recognize Me, I Am still there. Hence it is written, "Behold, I stand at the door and knock." This Divine Visitor, which is your True Self, and which is That Which I Am, is both the one who stands at the door and knocks, and the one who opens the door.

It is the glory of this recognition which has given to the enlightened true mastership. Do not look, then, for masters outside Me, nor mediators between yourself and Myself. There is but One Self, who needs no mediator. This Self is immediate, present and available. Any thought or belief which would seek to separate That Which I Am from that which you are, would be an illusion, no matter how lofty its concept nor how sacred its purpose. For it would seek to deny the ever-present I Am, the completeness of My Perfection, the God within you, the inspired thought back of your act.

21

Your True Self constitutes the only mediator between the visible and the Invisible. I Am that Self. Be still, then, and know that you are one with Me and My Being in you is your personality. It is also your body, mind and spirit. Every cell of your body, every thought of your mind, every glory of your spirit. Hence that which you have so ardently sought after has never been separated from you for one moment. My desire within you to be expressed has been the motivating Power, impelling and compelling you evermore to reach out, on and up.

I Am the Christ dwelling at the center of every soul. Human yet Divine; Infinite yet flowing through that which is apparently finite; unmanifest yet forever manifesting Myself; birthless and deathless yet forever being born; timeless, I Am forever creating time. And you, the expression of Myself, appear to be separated from Me merely because you are a unique personification of Myself. For I Am that personality which you are and which all people are. I Am in all and I Am all. When the recognition comes, within you, of this I Am Which I Am, you will have discovered your true Savior, your true Sonship and you will know that this Sonship is a projection of Myself, forever different from any other projection, immortal yet forever expanding.

Here you find the True Ideal, the Cosmic Pattern, the Eternal Friendship of the soul to itself, the God who is personified, the Person who is God-in-man. And how great is this Divine riddle! How inscrutable is the Sphinx! Truly, men have sought through the countless ages to solve this mystery—how can unity and multiplicity exist together without division? But now you have solved this mystery. You have compelled the Sphinx to answer her own question and she no longer devours you, but, like circumstance, must bow to that Divinity within you; like all created things, must acknowledge the supremacy of That Which I Am within you. This mystery of unity and multiplicity without division I have already proclaimed through the enlightened of the ages. But only the enlightened have understood My meaning; the unenlightened have not even realized that those who did understand Me were even as they. They thought that they were different, they believed them to be great prophets, great mediators, governed by invisible masters, controlled by those whom they have called saints.

22

But since I create both saint and sinner, know neither big nor little, good nor bad, and being ageless, since I create all ages, I am that which reveals and that which is revealed. And the stone which the builder rejected has become the chief stone of the corner, for the vulgar did not know that, which even the high priests failed to recognize, that the Ark of My Covenant was in the sanctuary of their own soul, that the Scroll of Life concealed in this Ark had inscribed on it merely these words: "I AM."

I AM THE ABUNDANCE WITHIN YOU

I Am come that you might have a more abundant life. To those who know not their true nature, believing themselves separated from good, I Am come. To those weary with disappointment and struggle who have sought life outside themselves, I point the way to certain salvation.

I Am in the midst of you is mighty to heal, to comfort, and to prosper. I have come to arouse you from your long dream of separation, from your night of despair. The dawn has come. The sun of truth rises over the horizon of ignorance. The light dissipates the darkness. The morning dew is upon the petals. They glisten in the sun. I Am that sun of truth dwelling within the sanctuary of your heart. I Am the morning star, guiding you to the manger of your salvation, wherein lies the child born from your own consciousness. This inner life is your only savior, the creator of your destiny, the arbiter of your faith.

Therefore, awake, become aware of My presence, for I Am life. I Am not something apart from your being. I Am your being. Closer than breathing, nearer than hands and feet, I Am. You have thought you denied My existence by affirming lack, fear and failure, but in reality you have merely affirmed My power to be to you that which you believed. I Am the Reality of your being, but I have always appeared to you in the form of your belief. I Am more than your conscious mind. I Am that which projects this mind which you call "you." I Am that which creates your personality and projects it from the center of My own Divine Originality.

I Am the Power which has bound you to your false belief. I Am the Presence which alone can give you freedom. Bondage and freedom are one

23

and the same. I Am, who is in the midst of your being, can project one as easily as the other. Bondage does not bind Me, it merely expresses Me. That which you call your bondage is really My freedom misused.

I have come to awaken you from the sense of limitation; to proclaim to you the eternal days of God-abundance. I have come to acquaint your mind with the truth, to convert your soul by reason, inspiration and illumination, to the realization that I Am is all there is, beside which there is none other. Within you is the secret place of the Most High, the Tabernacle of the Almighty, the Indwelling Good, the Ever-Present Father and the Eternal Child. This Ever-Present Father and this Eternal Child are one and the same Being. I Am that Being. I Am the All-Being. I Am your being. You are My Being. "I am that which thou art, thou art that which I am." Therefore, you may know that the Universal "I Am" is also the individual "I." Hence the individual "I" merges into the Universal "I Am"; is omnipotent wherever good impels the activities of Its thought. For the human thought is as Divine as is its consciousness of Reality, and the Omnipotent Law forever obeys its will.

If you can put aside your fear, doubt, and hurt which is but an expression of your sense of isolation; if you can put aside all negation and turn to Me alone, then you shall be made free. Be still and know that I Am God, your True Self. Be still and know that I Am the Life Principle. Be still and know that I Am the Truth, dispelling all error. I Am Power, neutralizing all weakness. I Am Abundance, swallowing up all lack. I Am your Real Self.

Nothing that you have ever said or done, no law that you have ever set in motion, is as great as I Am, for I transcend all uses of the Law. I, the Creator, re-create. I, the Molder, re-mold. I, the Maker, re-make. Therefore, you may trust what I shall do, for I Am God, the Living Spirit in the midst of you—not some-mighty, but All-Mighty. There is no law opposed to My Will. There is no opposite to My Nature. There is no darkness which My Light does not dissipate. There is no knowledge which I do not possess, for I Am Wisdom, the source of all knowledge. I Am Light, the source of all illumination. I Am Power, the source of all strength.

Therefore, be still and know that I Am the Creator and the thing cre-

V

ated. My Presence dissipates all apparent evil. Hence I have ever proclaimed, "Come unto me, all ye that labour and are heavy-laden, and I will give you rest."

I AM THE CREATIVENESS WITHIN YOU

Because I Am the Creativeness of the universe, and because My imagination is My creativeness, then you may know that to think is to create. Hence were the worlds formed by the power of My Word. Hence is your world formed by the power of My Word in you, for your word is My Word in you, your thought is My Thought in you, your power is My Power in you. I, the Universal, and you, the individual, are one and the same Being. I, the Universal, think in you, the individual, thus I the Universal endow you, the individual, with life, with creativeness—I Am that life and that creativeness within you.

"I Am the way, the truth and the life," means that the Infinite I, within the apparently finite you, is God. Thus your thought is creative. Thus your imagination projects form upon the screen of your experience. This is because I, the Creative Principle, dwell within you, projecting the law of My creativeness through your imagination. To know how to think is to know how to create, and this power to create through thought is the execution of My Will in you, the manifestation of My Being through you. This is My Image and Likeness manifest at the level of your consciousness. If you can consciously realize this, then you may know that I am still creating through your thinking.

I, the Universal, am now individual. I, the Impersonal, am now personal. And yet in My personality and individuality I still remain Universal, but I, the Universal Creative Mind, now become at the same time the individual and personal creative mind through your will, through your desire. Because you are some part of Me, you have the power to think and to create. This power is My Power, it is also your power, and because this is so, that which you have believed has come upon you, that which you have thought has transpired. Until now you have not known that the very power which binds you can give you freedom, that the very power which has created physical infirmities may also heal. I, the Eternal within, do all these things.

25

Because you believe that which you experience to be necessary, you perpetuate such experience. This also is My Mind working at the center of your being. "I Am" in the midst of you is the sole and only creative agency in the universe, whether that creative agency calls itself your imagination or My Will. It is one and the same. "I Am" in the midst of you can easily dissolve one creation and project another. The Master resides within and is never external. The picture is never the artist, the creation is never the creator. The Thinker existed before any particular thought, and when your present universe shall be rolled up like a scroll and numbered with the things once experienced, "I Am" will still be in the midst of you. You will remain and project another universe and yet another and beyond that more.

Neither your body, your environment, nor your mind are masters. You are the master of body, environment, and mind. They are your servants. They are My servants. Therefore they are your true servants when your thought is in harmony with beauty and at peace with Reality. You may permit Me to create a new experience for you, patterned after your own thought. But first you must have the idea of this better experience. You must conceive it in the silence of your imagination. This conception will be My Imagination working at the center of your being; My Will dominating yours, not dissolving it, but more fully expressing Myself through it, for My Will and your will are one and the same because all ideas finally come from Me.

You can have no ideas separate from Mine because you are that which I Am and I Am that which you are. You are Myself individualized. Your personality does not restrict me nor do I hinder it from expanding. Hence the joy of spontaneity and self-expression are real in you because they are real in Me. If you turn from fear to faith you will discover that fear has vanished and faith alone remains. If you turn from despair to certainty you will discover that weakness has fled and when you understand the subtle processes through which this transmutation has taken place, you will know that always you could have created one condition as easily as another. Always you have been the master of your fate.

26

I AM THE CHRIST WITHIN YOU

Be still and know that "I Am that which thou art and thou art that which I Am." Be still and know that I Am God within you. Be still and know that every atom of your body is in tune with Perfect Life. Be still and know that every organ of your body is in harmony with Me. Be still and know that every activity of your physical being moves in accord with my Divine Perfection. I Am the Principle of Perfection within you and I Am also the activity of that Principle, forever manifesting Myself in Perfect Form. I Am not caught in your body, but I Am your body. Never limited by its action, I produce its action.

By some divine intuition, by some inner whispering of your soul, by some light upon your path, you have progressed. I Am that light, that urge, that whisper, that voice.

I Am your real Self, the Christ within you proclaiming His Divine Presence to your human consciousness. This Christ within you is at the center of every person and every thing. Being the All Being, I Am the Being of all, from the smallest particle to the greatest, from the lowest form to the highest intelligence.

You must understand that this I Am, at the center of your being, is the I Am at the center of every man's being, of every animal's being, at the center of all being. When you do understand this, all nature will have a new meaning to you, for you will know that the odor of the rose is the radiation of My consciousness; you will know why the intelligence in the animal responds to you; you will understand the mystery of mysteries. You will possess the key which unlocks the storehouse of nature. You will be bound with an inseparable unity to all that exists. What you have called bondage is but a shadow, it is not a reality, for I Am your immortal self, your Divine being, unbound, unfettered and free.

The mind which you use is in reality your comprehension of Me at this present time. And yet I Am ever more than this comprehension, for your present experience is but a faint glimpse of My presence. Your limitation is My freedom expressed in a meager way. This Life Principle in you, which I Am, and this use of that which I Am by your intellect, seems to

contradict and deny My Universal Being, and yet, it really affirms My Being, of which you are a part.

Since all parts of Me are forever one with the wholeness of My Being, then that part which you are is never separated from My Being, but is forevermore united with It. Even the cells of your body are some part of this Being, one in consciousness with Me, and if you would be made whole, know that each cell of your body is in union with Me, has never been separated from Me, is forever at one with My Life. They have the consciousness of My Being and this consciousness of My Being alone constitutes Life.

You are the execution of My Will as I Am the One within you which conceives the purpose of that will. I Am the love, you are the beloved. I Am the abstract, you are the concrete. I Am the impersonal, you are the personal. There could be no you without Me. You as an individual are but one unique manifestation of My Being. Because My Being is in all people, each may recognize the other. I Am that which they recognize and I Am the intelligence which responds in each and through all.

This is the mystery of life, the enigma of the universe—how is it that I can remain Universal and still be individual? It is an understanding of this which has come to the great, which has led them back to the unity of the Whole, which has given them the power they possess. It is the awakening of this lesser self to the greater Self which is the New Birth. It is the surrender of the limited to the limitless, of the finite to the Infinite, and of restriction and bondage to freedom.

I, the Universal Self, multiply my Self-expression countlessly through My individual Selves. The soul of you and of all, the imperishable part of all, is a different manifestation, a unique expression of Myself. The understanding of this is the key to the mystery of life which unlocks the hidden treasures of My Being—this consciousness of Oneness, this knowledge that the Universal I Am is also the individual I, this recognition that "the highest God and the innermost God is OneGod." To know this is to know the Truth which makes you free.

You must know that the infinite creativity of My Nature, the limitless creativeness of My Imagination, projecting My Substance within the void,

giving form to the formless, that this inner imagination is the final, sole and only creative agency in the universe. You must realize that this Creative Power which I Am is also the Creative Power which you are, for you and I are One.

I AM THE SUSTAINER WITHIN YOU

Nothing is or can be unless it be some expression of My Life and Intelligence. In the heart of each I live; at the center of all creation I dwell. I fill all space. I Am All-in-All, over all and through all. Being the One Infinite Reality, I create and control. There is no personality, no individuality, separated from me, since I Am the Essence and the Life of each and all. Infinite and impersonal, I Am still personified.

The illusion which you suffer and the grief you bear are not because you are separated from Me, but because you do not realize that you are forever united with Me, for I am at the center of your being; and being that which you are, I Am forever personifying Myself in you. At the center of your comprehending mind, I, the All, the Infinite, the Impersonal, am individualized and personified. Therefore the "I Am" which speaks is the real you, your true Self. From the mightiest form to the smallest atom, in you and in all—in the animal, vegetable and mineral kingdoms—My Intelligence projects all. My Power envelops all. My Life animates all.

You are not merely a shadow of Myself; you are the Substance of Me. You are My Mind in action, the enforcement of My Law, the Law of your own Divinity. This Law of your Divinity is both freedom and bondage, even as you use It, for my Law reflects to you the images of your own thought. Bondage and limitation, joy and grief are one to Me. They are merely different manifestations of the eternal expressions of Myself, for I Am not a dualism, but a Unity.

I Am not little in one place and big in another. I Am not good in one place and evil in another. I Am above big and little, good and evil, just as I transcend time and space, yet I Am in you, creating what you call time and space, sickness and health, happiness and misery, good and evil. When you awake to the realization of that which I Am in the midst of you, from the very substance of impoverishment you will enrich yourself. Sitting in the presence of confusion you will be at peace, where the fires of hell

29

burn not, for they are consumed by a greater passion. They are extinguished by the reversal of your own thought, for "Behold, I Am in the midst of you" creates heaven and hell, condemns and saves, gives birth to Adam and Christ, is the seeker and that which is sought after. Behold, I Am the See-er and the thing seen.

I Am within you, then, is the Creator and Sustainer. I Am the One who projects My imagination upon the screen of your experience and the images of My thought are manifest throughout all creation. Creation is nothing other than an image of My thought. But you are not an image of My thought. You are My thought, for you and I are One, not two. You are My thought personified; through you I, the Timeless, enter into time; I, the Formless, take form; I, the Impersonal, become personal.

Thus, all ideas, all desires, all thoughts, come from Me, for I Am all there is. If you listen deeply to yourself, you are listening to Me. Your mind becomes illumined because I Am light. Your mind knows, because I Am knowledge. Your thought is the enforcement of My Law, because My Law is your thought. This is why it is that your thought is creative. Even though you have misused this gift of Life, you have never changed its nature nor destroyed its purpose. All your desires are basically good, and the Divine Urge within you which impels you toward self-expression is My Nature, the irresistible desire within Me to become self-expressed through you.

Every event that has ever transpired, all human history, are but different imprints of my thought, creating as they do time, space, and circumstance. I Am both cause and effect. I Am all processes between cause and effect, therefore the "I Am" in you remains forever unconditioned by any existing form; is never bound to any outline or to any particular experience; has come through no processes of evolution whatsoever. That which you call evolution is but the manner of My Self-expression. That which you call unfoldment is but an ever-awakening consciousness within you of My Presence, for My Presence covers all, pervades all, and animates all.

"I Am that I Am," beside which there is no other Presence, no other animating Principle. I Am your omnipresent Self. Wherever you look you will see Me. Wherever you go you will find Me.

YOUR INVISIBLE
POWER

●

PART IV

VI

GOD
THE SELF-EVIDENT TRUTH
WITHIN YOU

Part IV

T IS self-evident that we live. As Descartes said, "I think, therefore I am." This might be called an axiom of reason whereby one perceives that he exists. An axiom of reason is a truth so self-evident, so universally experienced, so immediately known to the mind that reason cannot deny its existence. That there are such final truths no one doubts.

We wish to establish our identity in the universe, the limitless possibility of self-expression, and the certainty of eternal unfoldment. We wish to establish identity, individuality, unity, completion.

Our first self-evident proposition is, that the Truth is that which is. We are using Truth in the sense of Its absolute meaning—not some truth, or a truth, but the Truth, the ultimate Reality. The Truth, being that which is, must include all that was, is, or ever shall be. And being that which is, and being all that is, there can be nothing unlike It, different from It, nor opposed to It.

While it is true that our present finite comprehension does not grasp such an infinity, and while it is equally true that appearance seems to contradict this fundamental premise, we may be certain that even the judgment of the senses is no final criterion. The earth and the sky do not finally meet anywhere. We all have such apparent horizons attached to our experience. But we must postulate an absolute, unconditioned Truth somewhere. This is the Truth Jesus referred to when he said, "Ye shall know the truth and the truth shall make you free." What this Truth is, and how It operates through us, is the nature of our inquiry.

That which reason cannot doubt, that to which the essence of reason can find no opposite, but which clear thinking must have complete confidence in—by the very fact of its inability to conceive an opposite—that is Truth.

31

The Bible tells us, "For by thy words thou shalt be justified, and by thy words thou shalt be condemned." The concept of Truth formulated in our thought becomes our word, becomes our affirmation of our relationship to the universe. For instance, we either believe that God is all there is or we do not believe that God is all there is.

If clear reasoning does deliver the perception of the allness of Truth, and if Truth is a synonym for God, then we may say: God is all there is. And we may add that it is impossible to conceive any opposite, otherness, difference, unlikeness, either in what we call the past (which is memory), in what we call the present (which is experience), or in what we call the future (which is anticipation). For past, present and future is but a continuity upon which is threaded the sequence of experience.

If God is all there is, then past, present and future; time, experience and form, if they exist at all, must exist as some part of Truth. If this Truth is all there is, then we also must be included in It, and we should identify ourselves with It. Thus the allness of Truth automatically includes the reality of our own being.

We arrive next at the conclusion that Truth, being all there is, must be universal. That is, Spirit plus nothing equals Spirit. Since there is no such thing as that which is not, a lie merely becomes a denial of Truth. A lie has no validity, no power, remaining merely a suppositional opposite to that which of itself is positive, absolute and eternal. Truth is universal. Cancelling what is not and leaving what is, we arrive at the conclusion that nothing has ever happened to the Truth. It was not born, It will not die. It did not come, It will not go. It has no degrees of being. It is universally present.

Thus we arrive at the conclusion that Truth is indivisible. Having nothing unlike It, with which to divide It, being all, It remains a complete unity. Therefore, every announcement of being is an announcement of Truth. The indivisible wholeness of Truth includes all that really is, and since I can say, "I am," Truth includes myself.

Emerson tells us that no power of genius has ever yet had the smallest success in explaining existence. The perfect enigma remains. Truth is not explained, nor is It explainable. Our unity with It is not something which

we acquire. It is a reality which we discover. This is a conclusion at which we arrive, not by intellectual processes alone, because the genius of the intellect has never explained its own existence, it has merely experienced it. If the Truth is all there is, if It is universal and a unit, then nothing came before It and nothing came after It, but Itself was, is, and remains, all. The indivisibility of Truth guarantees Its unity and Its unity guarantees not only our oneness with It and Its oneness with us, but the inseparable allness of this one-ness. Transcendent, even while it is immanent. The Truth unifies transcendence and immanence. The perceiver and the thing perceived are united in one common Mind and Existence.

Something cannot be divided by nothing. If the Truth is all there is, and if there is nothing unlike It, then there is no dividing line between God and man. Hence the self-evident perception of Jesus when he said, "The Father and I are one." Such all-ness announces independence. That which we call the attributes of Truth are not attributes of something which projects such alleged attributes, but are activities of that which constitutes such attributes. Essence and performance are identical. Truth and attribute are one. This must have been what Jesus had in mind when he said, "The words I speak unto you, they are spirit and they are life." He was not thinking of his word reflecting or transmitting some overdwelling power, but that Power Itself was undivorced from the word. His word was that Power, not merely an expression or an extension of It. The attribute was the essence. Hence Power is never separated from Itself and the Mind which conceived the cosmos, giving birth to its infinite forms, is identified with the plot in the latest play—the same Mind, because all Mind is One.

Within all people and within everything that lives there is an impulsion toward self-expression. This impulse is dynamic and irresistible. The very fact that there is an insistent urge for self-expression in all individuals proves that this urge is cosmic because the apparent parts substantiate the characteristics of the universal wholeness, if our axiom of Unity is correct. Therefore, the desire for self-expression is not only legitimate, it is irresistible. To seek escape from this desire would be an unconscious attempt toward self-annihilation. Each individual must interpret the universe for

himself, since he has to interpret it to himself. The universe can interpret itself for him only by interpreting itself to him, through him. God can give us only what we take, and the taking is the self-expression of God in us—not something else, something other, or different from God, not something which has succeeded in passing a dividing line, but itself is God.

The urge, then, which causes us to say "I am," is more than an urge causing us to express a Power which extends Itself through us or an Intelligence which uses us as an instrument for Its activity. This urge in us which causes us to say "I am" is God. Hence our self-awareness is Its self-awareness. This perception of unity has been basic to the spiritual genius of the ages and is but another way of saying that God is all there is. The enigma of unity is solved in such degree as one perceives unity in multiplicity and multiplicity in unity.

We are using this illustration of axioms, not to confuse nor to mystify, but to show that through all of the attempts which ever have been made to teach the Truth, this one central theme has run—the indivisible unity of God and man. Every sacred literature of the ages contains it. The ancient Jewish faith proclaimed it when, in the Sixth Chapter of Deuteronomy, Moses said, "Hear, O Israel, the Lord our God is one Lord," and Jesus when he said, "The Father that dwelleth in me, he doeth the works."

To realize that this Indivisible Wholeness is at the center of our own being is to understand that the power of our individual word is an activity of the Infinite and Eternal I Am, the Everlasting and Perfect Spirit. That Spirit in us, is us. No greater unity could be delivered than that which, by the very nature of being, cannot be withheld. This deliverance is not partial, but complete.

Next we arrive at another self-evident proposition, which is that the Truth is unchangeable. This is self-evident since there is nothing for the Truth to change into. It cannot change into nothing because there is no such thing as nothing. It cannot change into Itself because It already is Itself. It remains, persistent, permanent. It was this perception that caused Emerson to say that no moment in eternity is any better than the present one, and the New Testament Prophet to exclaim, "Beloved, now are we

the sons of God." Jesus stood in the midst of passing human events, and proclaimed that the Kingdom of Heaven is at hand, or within man.

If the Truth cannot change, if It is permanent, if It is ever-present, then It is always reliable. There is nothing but stability and nothing but security. The Truth is faithful. Truth has neither birth, evolution nor decay. Because the Truth is eternal and changeless, and because I exist, and because that which I am is It in me, it is self-evident that I am eternal. Such is the perception of immortality, deathlessness and everlasting being. This is but another way of saying that God cannot die, that God is all there is, that God is the essence of my life and is my life; that I am an immortal and an eternal being now.

We next arrive at a conclusion which tends to liberate the mind from the thralldom of circumstances. The Truth, being all there is, is both cause and effect. It is self-evident that Truth has no cause and that there is no effect external to It. Therefore, cause and effect are one and the same thing. There is neither cause nor effect external to Truth. Hence, any belief in the cause and effect of bondage has no substantiality, for if it did bondage would be permanent, changeless and inescapable. If Truth were bondage, freedom would be unthinkable. The Truth which sets us free is not the introduction of some higher power on a lower plane. It is the knowledge that there are no higher and no lower planes in Truth, no higher and no lower laws in Truth. There is merely what is and the self-action of what is proclaiming Itself to be that which It is. If Truth were bondage instead of freedom, then the very knowledge of Truth would create more bondage. But since the Truth is freedom then a knowledge of Truth is freedom. Hence, to know the Truth is to be free. Truth and freedom are identical.

Cause and Effect, therefore, becomes a plaything, a something to be used. Karma and Kismet become bubbles to be blown about. Such is the perception of power. Such is the realization that the knowledge of Truth is power. Power is that which compels, necessitates, authorizes, commands. "He (Jesus) taught them as one having authority and not as the scribes." This was because he understood the nature of the spontaneous Spirit within him and realized that the Law of Cause and Effect is

35

merely the mechanical method through which the Word of Power proves Its authority.

We arrive next at the perception of person, individuality, personality, and humanity, for again we may say, "I think, therefore I am." Also our fellowman may say, "I think, therefore I am." The allness of Truth delivers this message, that in a certain sense each is all, because of the indivisibility of Truth, and all is in each. Such is the mystery of individuality, which the mask of personality but dimly reveals. The Truth, being all, means that each individual is forced to be Truth and nothing but Truth. Truth does not deny individuality, personality, nor humanity. It affirms that each exists in his apparently separate star, maintaining an eternal, changeless and perfect identity in the allness of good. Each is an individualized expression of the One.

There is nothing which separates one individual from another, even while there is nothing which can annihilate, subtract from or add to the individuality of each. Such totality in individuality and such individuality in totality is perceived, not so much by an intellectual process as by the very axiom itself which delivers the necessity of accepting the Principle of Omnipresence.

This Principle of Omnipresence also declares the Principle of Omniscience. Truth is not only all-presence, It is all-knowledge. It is because this is so that an inventor may say, "I know the answer to my problem;" the author can say, "My plot is worked out;" the organizer can say, "My organization is complete." By consciously practicing Omnipotence, Omniscience and Omnipresence, we prove in some measure that these self-evident abstractions are real necessities, reliable, substantial and available. We need, then, labor under no illusion that it is necessary to deny individuality, personality or humanity in order to affirm the allness of God; for such is the perception of unity.

But if Truth is all there is, then Truth is Intelligence, Truth is what we call Mind, Truth is Idea. Idea becomes absolute. Idea reflects experience. The allness of Idea destroys the belief in any physical, mental or material universe external to concept. Creation becomes the contemplation of Truth. Such is the perception of creativeness. Forms are real but not

self-sustained, they are nothing in themselves. There is nothing in such a reflected idea to have control even over itself.

Having established unity, indivisibility, permanence, power, Omniscience, Omnipresence and Omnipotence, we arrive at the conclusion of eternal dominion. It is self-evident that if the objective world were a thing in itself and we were in no way connected with it, other than by experiencing it as an external fact, then we could not possibly exercise dominion. The Truth would be in fragments, which we should never be able to put together; hence we never could attain wholeness. The greatest teachings of the ages contradict the fragmentary theory and insist on resolving all apparent multiplicity into a final unity. This unity is not some far-off event, but a present fact. Modern science tends in the same direction.

This allness of Truth, stated in the simplest manner, affirms that God is all there is. God never changes. God is in me. God is that which I am. God is in the universe. God is the universe.

At first man is ignorant of his true nature. The Word has become flesh, but self-conscious life has not yet emerged. The fusion of will, desire and volition, without which there can be no personality, has not taken place. Finally the Word not only becomes flesh, it also becomes person. Man awakes to life, turns toward the light and triumphs over limitation.

Therefore, our final self-evident proposition delivers the perception of bliss, wholeness and perfection. The universal I Am and the individual I are One in peace, joy, love, wisdom, beauty and power.

In the beginning was the Word, and the Word was Life, and the Word
was Law, and the Word was Light; and the Light through Law
produced form; and the created form turned to the Light;
and the Light of consciousness dawned; and man
beheld the Light and walked in It; and
the Light was All.

VII

CPSIA information can be obtained at www.ICGtesting.com
Printed in the USA
BVOW02s1433011013

332493BV00008B/38/P